HOW TO IMPRESS JESUS

Join his adventures in this world and beyond.

G. Stempien Publishing Company

ISBN 978-0-939472-51-1

Editorial offices in New Quay, Wales, UK

All photos are National Archives or public domain

This book is dedicated to the memory of Charles Martel (the Hammer) who in 722 A.D. saved all of Europe and probably the world for Christianity.

LIST OF CONTENTS

Pre-Introduction

Why are vultures so important in this book? Because they eat carrion and they would have been among the disappointed when they discovered that Jesus arose from the dead and that he did not leave a body - or food - behind for them.

It would seem that it is time for all vultures to convert.

INTRODUCTION

You are about to read a one-of-a-kind book about Christianity. It is written to describe Jesus and his teachings in a wonderfully entertaining way.

HOW TO IMPRESS JESUS is written for all age levels, basically from 5 to 109. But this book will also be useful reading for anyone of any age who wants to learn more about Christianity or to refresh what he already knows. This book is unusual in that way. The basics are here. So too are the unusual, described so that all can understand.

There is nothing sacrilegious (anti-Jesus) in this book. It does not poke fun at Jesus and certainly does not have ANY lewd (unclean) observations. But the author does have fun with Jesus, in a playful way, all the while with the thought in mind: "What would Jesus think of this?" Especially if children are watching.

Everything in this book is based on the revised King James Version of the New and Old Testaments. There aren't any surprise doctrines or crazy beliefs. This is basic Christianity, made to be entertaining and for all.

The author is a devout Christian which is meant to imply that you will find standard Christianity in these pages. No single denominational approach is presented. As Christians, we all share the same basic beliefs and that is what is discussed within these pages. Jesus is our Lord and Saviour!

The only thing out-of-the-ordinary about this book is the style of presentation which is both of it's own kind, but logical and biblically correct.

LAUGHTER IN HEAVEN

This book starts off with a discussion of the sense of humour of Jesus because some people claim that there is no room for humour in religion. But would those same people say the same thing if they knew that Jesus Himself displayed a very active sense of humour?

Did Jesus have a sense of humour? A lot of people have asked this question. There is a lot of evidence that the Lord did have a rather good sense of humour, although it might be characterised as a wry (or dry) type of humour.

What is wry humour? It is the type based more on the unexpected than outright joke telling. Jesus also is a master at puns.

Jesus could also be <u>almost</u> sarcastic at times. A perfect example was the time when Our Lord was heading toward the tomb of Lazarus and told everyone that Lazarus was just sleeping. Many people laughed at Jesus in ridicule for such a statement; but Jesus of course knew better. It was as if he were making fun in advance of the people who were laughing at him and could give them a big "I told you so," after raising Lazarus. Jesus omitted the "I told you so" afterward.

Another example of the humour of Jesus was when he gave Peter control of His church (Matthew 16:18). What did he tell Peter: that he was the rock upon which he would build his church. What made this funny is that the word that Jesus used for Rock was the same as our current day "Rocky" as in the famous movie.

Still, why is this funny? Because Peter was anything but a strong armed, powerful fighter but more of a person who wasn't too sure of himself. Although Peter was totally loyal he was really not a "Rocky" however.

In slang, Jesus was "funnin'" with Peter and the other apostles but also deadly serious in putting the man he trusted most at the top of his church.

There are many examples of the humour of Jesus. When he was discussing the spreading of his teachings with the apostles, Jesus asked them this question: "Does anyone bring a lamp home and put it under the bed or under a washtub?" It's an absurdly funny picture the Saviour painted. Imagine someone doing that! But he sure got his point across. With humour! Jesus really was supremely funny!

When someone asks you for bread would you hand him a snake? What a picture that presents! And it was a question asked by Jesus to teach another lesson to show that the Father only gives good things to his Children. I wish I'd had him teaching in my school.

Jesus could be edgy, too. Consider the time when a non-Israeli woman came to him for help with her daughter who was possessed of a devil. Jesus at first **faked** condescension, saying, "It is not right to take the children's bread and toss it to the dogs," meaning that the people of his own race and beliefs should come first, not hers. He was testing her not being mean.

But the woman, sensing his true self, replied, "Yes Lord, but even the dogs under the table eat the children's crumbs."

Jesus must've smiled at that. And, yes, he did remove the demon from the woman's daughter.

How can anyone doubt that Jesus used humour in his ministry? Some people call it unexpected humour, some call it dry humour some call it a masterful use of puns; maybe it could best be described as divine wit!

What about the sense of humour of God the Father? How does he rate as a comedian? Some people might answer by saying: "Well, he made man, didn't he?" But that's an ancient joke.

But God's sense of humour is noted in the Old Testament in several spots, particularly Psalms 59:8 where it is written: But Thou, Oh Lord, dost laugh at them; Thou dost hold all nations in derision.

Based on Scriptural evidence, it seems pretty clear that both God the Father and God the Son have streaks of humour in them. The Holy Ghost, however, seems to be somewhat less inclined to humour, although it seemed that he was bordering on the slapstick when he broke in on the apostles like he did on Pentecost.

There can be very little doubt that God approves of humour. Examine Proverbs 17:22, "A merry heart doeth good like a medicine." In fact, Proverbs is filled with many light hearted offerings meant to make you smile.

And has anyone really considered the first three words of the Bible...In the beginning? Could this be a code telling us that God is a baseball fan and had been one before baseball even existed? Could "In the beginning..." translate to "In the big inning?" when it all started? (Noted by famous baseball announcer Jack Brickhouse)

Jesus is missing!

An APB (all Points Bulletin, or search) has been in effect for Jesus Christ for the past 2000 years. He was last seen being crucified by the Romans around the year 33 A.D. and has not been seen since, leaving an empty tomb behind while it is said that he arose to heaven.

Rumours persist that he had arisen from the dead and gone to heaven to join his Father and the Holy Ghost. However, it is also widely believed that the Holy Ghost - alias the Comforter - has frequently been seen on Earth and in the vicinity of the planet, continuing the work that has been begun by Jesus Christ.

Descriptions of Jesus vary. He is generally described as an average-sized Semitic male - possibly Armenian, probably of Jewish lineage - and sporting shoulder length brownish hair and a full beard. He is best known for curing the sick, expelling demons and preaching a doctrine of peace and love of one's fellow man.

There is also an APB on the Holy Ghost who is wanted for questioning in regard to the whereabouts of Jesus. The Holy Ghost - aka The Comforter - is usually depicted as a white dove-like bird with the ability to fly directly through solid objects. His modus operandi (method of operation) is to hover upon unsuspecting individuals and endow them with great spiritual and intellectual knowledge.

Anyone who has knowledge of these two beings - or potentially one being in the form of two - is asked to contact the currently reigning pope as soon as possible and make a full confession.

The conversion of Vultures

By their very nature, vultures have an anti-social view of the world. Most vultures are atheists. They believe in nothing but locating their next meal.

However, some vultures are more curious than others. Not long ago, a missionary cardinal had been sent to Tunisia with the hope of converting the vulture population to Christianity.

While it is a very slow process, some signs of progress have been reported. Hence, the following conversation between two potential avian (bird like) converts is provided for inspiration to demonstrate the power of witnessing for the Lord.

The vultures are named Mack and Jane and they are bird and wife.

MACK: I'm not quite sure yet what I think about this Jesus person.

JANE: Yes, it is all pretty hard to take in for bird brains like us.

MACK: True, but one of the main figures in Christianity is a bird, something like us.

JANE: You mean the Holy Ghost. Yeah, knowing about him makes me feel a lot better about Christianity.

MACK: But there's something else I REALLY LIKE about Christianity, at least some forms of it.

JANE: What's that?

MACK: It's the idea of eating the body and drinking the blood of Jesus, their main god.

JANE: I know what you mean. That really appeals to me, too.

MACK: They don't just talk about eating him one time, but somehow eating him again and again.

JANE: Phew! That's a mystery that's beyond me.

MACK: I guess that's where faith comes in, huh?

JANE: I hope that the Holy Ghost can some day explain things to us. That is supposed to be his job, you know.

MACK: I'm kind of scared of ghosts, though. He might be scary.

JANE: I'm pretty confused about him, too. I mean, if he's supposed to be a dove, why is he called a Holy Ghost?

MACK: Well, I figure he could be the ghost of a dove.

JANE: Hey, that's a good idea.

MACK: I just spotted the minister's car coming down the road. Let's see if he's having a service today. He's Anglican.

JANE: But just don't expect to eat any of those host things today. They don't just pass them out to anyone, you know.

Thus, the near-converts flew off. We will keep in touch with them to see how well their learning of the faith progresses.

THE MANY HATS OF JESUS

There aren't any drawings of Jesus wearing hats. There aren't any photographs of Jesus wearing hats. No one ever mentioned if Jesus ever wore a hat. Does this mean that Jesus was a man without a hat? Not necessarily.

For all we know, Jesus could have been a hat lover. Let's take a look at how Jesus might have appeared sporting an appropriate hat for an appropriate activity. No one can deny that Our Lord was a man of many hats as the saying goes.

Jesus didn't have a lot of money, so he didn't drive around in cabs or buses and he never took the train anywhere. Of course, none of these forms of transportation existed at that time which is another reason Jesus never used any of them. Maybe he takes this type of transportation today, but nobody seems to have seen him.

Jesus walked a lot. Most of the time, really. Often in the desert. Is it possible that on these walks he wore a pith helmet?

A pith helmet (for deserts) would be a very useful piece of headgear while heading toward the marriage ceremony where Jesus was later to become famous for changing water into wine. JOHN 2:1-11.

Most people know the story of how Jesus, his mother Mary and some of the apostles had been invited to a wedding in Cana, which was a small but centrally located town in Galilee. By the way, it's been pointed out that they were invited not because they were boring and humourless but for quite the opposite reasons.

The wedding party had run out of wine too early and so at his mother's request, Jesus performed the miracle of changing water into wine.

This was of particular importance because it was the first miracle that Jesus performed. The general belief was that he had been reluctant to perform this first miracle and that he finally did it as a special favour to his mother.

And it was time for Jesus to change hats again. Would he exchange his pith helmet for a magician's hat?

But, of course, these weren't just magic tricks that Jesus was performing. Tricks are simple deceptions of an audience. Genuine miracles are acts that go against the laws of nature like: turning one substance into another substance by the wave of a hand or by a simple spoken command.

It isn't recorded anywhere whether or not Jesus could swim. He did seem to spend a lot of time around water: baptizing people, fishing, walking on water, finding disciples, and riding in boats during heavy thunderstorms, for example. But no one has ever reported him swimming or high diving from a board.

It seems that Jesus preferred to walk on water as opposed to swimming in it or diving into it. He must have been very light on his feet.

It was right after Jesus had performed another miracle - feeding thousands of people with two fishes and five loaves - that he told his disciples to head to the Sea of Galilee where he'd meet them soon. MATT 14:15-22).

Sometime later, Jesus caught up to the apostles but found that they were already at sea. It is at this point that Jesus donned another one of his hats - a cool captain's cap - and did this particular stroll upon the water (there were other ones), to the shock of the apostles.

Keeping the brim low over his eyes to keep out the surging water thrown up by the spray, Jesus at first was unrecognizable to the apostles. Thinking he was a ghost, Peter called out to him for assurance. Then the Lord told Peter to walk out onto the water to meet him.

Peter did as instructed, leaving the safety of the boat despite the cries from the other apostles. After treading water for a short while, Peter became suddenly terrified and called to Jesus for help. Jesus obliged, taking Peter's hand to keep him from sinking. Then they got into the boat together.

But there was another time when Jesus and the apostles were caught in an even worse storm. The Lord and the apostles had just departed the town of Capernaum where Jesus had spent the day healing crowds of people.

They boarded their awaiting craft and Jesus, tired from the day's activity, immediately fell asleep. The ship set to sea and a wild storm erupted. At first the apostles didn't want to bother Jesus, but then they began to fear for their safety and decided to call on him for help. (MATT 8:23-26)

Jesus got to work and faced the storm.

This could've been the only hat he had with him at the time, a fun beach hat. But it did the job and after Jesus rebuked the winds and the sea the storm let up and he could finally get back to sleep!

Jesus may have worn his strangest hat on a special trip he made to Bethany. This was where a man named Lazarus lived. We heard of him earlier. Lazarus was gravely ill. Knowing of the powers that Jesus had, the sisters of Lazarus sent for Jesus so he might cure their stricken brother.

Lazarus died by the time that Jesus arrived. Jesus was distraught and was greatly moved by the anguish of those who loved Lazarus. It seemed pretty clear that Jesus had been looking forward to visiting Lazarus, maybe to play a card game of hearts or whist with him. Or maybe even a game of checkers, who knows? Lazarus was good company.

Jesus was despondent at his sudden loss. And he determined to do something about it as no one else could do something about it. He then performed one of his greatest miracles - raising Lazarus from the dead. (JOHN 11: 42-46).

Jesus might have put on a mortician (grave digger's) hat for this great deed.

No, this is not the magician's hat or a common top hat. It is an undertaker's hat and can be identified as such by the broad ribbon wound around its base.

Lazarus of course was raised from the dead.

JUST IMAGINE HOW LAZARUS MUST HAVE FELT!

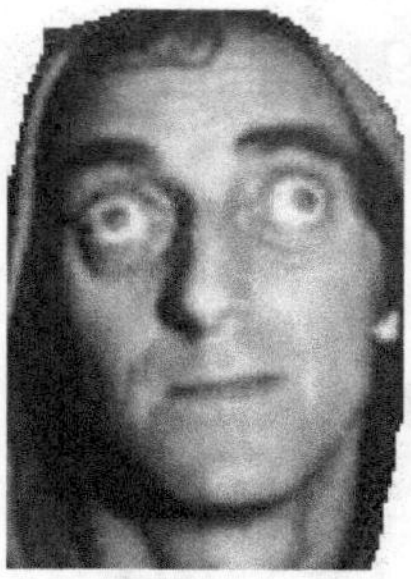

"That must be you out there...Jesus?"

(thanks to the great actor Marty Feldman's impersonation. Seen in "Young Frankenstein")

It is rumoured that because of the raising of Lazarus from the dead that certain non-Christian localities wanted to make note of their pagan beliefs where the dead do not come back to bother them. One way they did this was by posting the following type of warning next to their multiple Chamber of Commerce Signs:

Jesus usually walked, either on land or on water. He also travelled by water in the more conventional way, using a boat. Jesus didn't often use beasts of burden - donkeys, camels, horses - to get around. But on his triumphal Palm Sunday entrance into Jerusalem an ass seemed appropriate. Jesus would want a fitting piece of headgear, too, so he might choose a gaucho hat - a red one!

After all, it was a festive occasion and so Jesus would feel like being a little flashy.

This was the first Palm Sunday, the day in which Jesus was widely hailed as a messiah and had his path strewn with palms. Things changed pretty importantly by the end of the week (Holy Week). But at least this one day had a joyous feel to it. (JOHN 12: 12-18) Good Friday was not so fun, of course.

Many of the people in the Palm Sunday crowd had also attended the raising of Lazarus. Many others in the crowd had heard of the miracle, and it was also because of this that so many more accepted Jesus and worshipped the Lord this day.

There are even unconfirmed reports that later Jesus and some of the apostles had a good natured palm frond fight! Reportedly, Judas left in a huff.

By this time, though, Jesus had made a lot of enemies. These were mostly among the upper classes and the bankers and high priests. Jesus had a direct encounter with these powerful people one day when he was heading to the temple.

Jesus might have thought that for this occasion he should find something conservative to wear on his head. So he could have grabbed a feathered homburg from one of the haberdashers selling wares in the temple where they should not have been.

Jesus wasn't too happy about the mob that had taken over the temple. In fact, he marched through the aisles, pushing over tables and tossing out the people who were desecrating the holy place. (LUKE 19: 45-47).

Quoting Jesus: **"It is written. My house is the house of prayer: but ye have made it a den of thieves."**

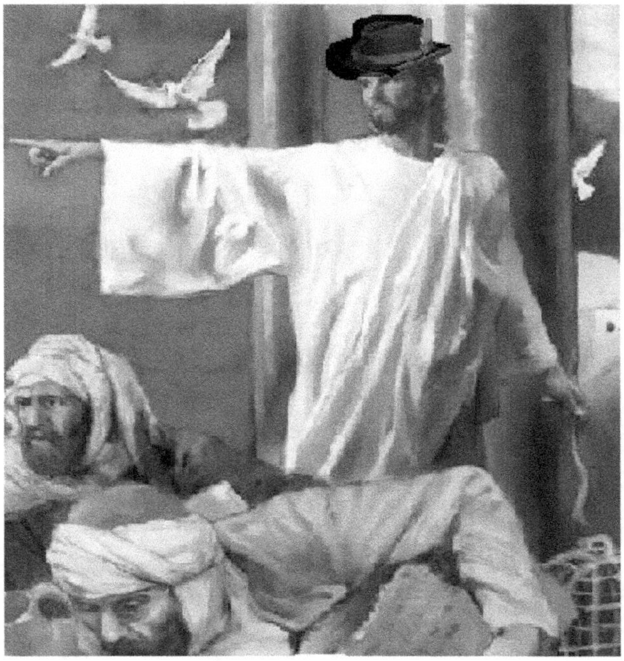

Jesus is a banking examiner (cop) no one wants to see at his door! Imagine trying to trick him about the money you've been stealing!

The Last Supper was only a few days away now.

The Last Supper. No one wore a hat.

THE PARABLES OF JESUS

RETURN OF THE VULTURES, MACK & JANE

MACK: Hey, let's find a place to roost.

JANE: Yeah, my tail feather's dragging.

Mack and Jane had just been speaking to their cardinal friend about the parables that Jesus used to teach his disciples. They were confused.

MACK: Phew, that Jesus sure used to tell a lot of parables!

JANE: I think we could use some help trying to figure them out. Ah, here he comes now.

MACK: Oh, it's Mortimer. That's one smart vulture!

Their friend Mortimer then joins Mack and Jane, settling onto a nearby limb.

MORT: Hi, Mack and Jane. I hear you're a little confused about the parables Jesus used to tell the apostles.

JANE: More than confused: we're conposculated.

MORT: Huh, never heard that word before.

MACK: Say, Mort, where did an old vulture like you learn so much about Jesus?

MORT: I was in overeaters anonymous with a capuchin monkey. It turned out that the capuchin was studying to be a Catholic by aping one of the attendants. How did you two get involved?

MACK: I got stuck in the bush one day with a couple of cardinals during a big thunderstorm.

JANE: Yeah, those cardinals sure like to preach.

MORT: So, what can I help you buzzards with?

JANE: These parables of Jesus. We can't quite figure them out.

MORT: Any in particular.

MACK: Yes! The one about the vultures.

MORT: I know that one well. It's one of the lesser known of the parables, however.

JANE: Can you recite it for us?

MORT: Sure, it's an easy one to remember. **"Where the body is, there the vultures will be gathered together."** **(LUKE 17:37)**

MACK: Now that's a parable that a vulture can sink a beak into.

JANE: But what does it really mean?

MORT: Well, it's very good for vultures. It points out the fact that vultures are attracted to carrion.

JANE: True. With or without ketchup and mustard.

MORT: And it's a very natural thing for vultures to be attracted to carrion. It's something that should and will happen. So, in his parable, Jesus is telling the people that certain things are inevitable and they should be on guard for them to happen.

MACK: Can you give us an example?

MORT: Yes. In this particular parable, Jesus was saying that he will come again because it is the will of God. It is inevitable, but it may come when you least expect it. So be ready.

JANE: That's right. It is just like us, sitting up there on our perches, waiting for something to come our way...food wise.

MACK: I'm getting kind of hungry with all this talk of food.

JANE: Me. too. You know, I just spotted a snack down below. What if we go grab something to eat and continue our lesson?

MORT: That sounds good to me. I'm getting a little hungry myself.

So the three novice Christian vultures left their perches to resume their talks while they dined.

But suddenly they saw a fourth vulture heading toward them, almost as if to give truth to the parable about the vultures. But he was a faithless bird.

MACK: Oh, oh - here comes Dirk.

MORT: I don't think I know Dirk.

JANE: He's a loud-mouthed slob. Doesn't believe in God or anything else.

MORT: Let's see if we can convince him.

DIRK: Hey, you pigs, save some for me.

MACK: Go away, Dirk. There's better feeding about a mile north of here.

DIRK: Ha, I know where the feeding's good.

MORT: How about that, a parable come to life before your eyes.

DIRK: Parable? Parable? What are you talking about?

JANE: We were talking about the parables of Jesus.

DIRK: Must we? While I'm eating?

MACK: Are you afraid you might learn something positive?

DIRK: No, I'm afraid I'll be bored to death.

MORT: Well, we're the one's to eat you then.

JANE: Dirk, we're going to continue with our lesson with or without you.

DIRK: Fine, I'll try not to choke.

MACK: Okay, Mort, this parable is the one that confuses me more than any other. It's the one about the man who went on a journey and left his servants some money to take care of for him. One got five talents, or dollars, the other two and the other just one.

MORT: Right, and when the master got back he was happy with this servants who increased the number of dollars he'd given them by investing them wisely. But he was angry with the servant who only hid the money and gave the master his one buck back when he returned.

MACK: That sounds to me like Jesus is saying that it is really important to amass as much wealth as you can. I always thought Jesus was more concerned with promoting his Father's kingdom, not an earthly one.

MORT: Yes, I can see how you'd be confused. Your problem is that you took the message exactly as said. What Jesus meant was that he expects us to use the abilities given us to their fullest potential. He was cautioning against indifference and idleness. The life of a Christian shouldn't be one of standing pat but of ever striving to serve the Lord.

JANE: Yes! It's kind of like that saying: "The Lord helps those who help themselves."

MORT: And like so many of those proverbs, that one is absolutely correct!

JANE: Okay, now I've got one for you that has really been bothering me. It's about the owner of the vineyard who paid all of his help the same no matter how long they worked. I don't get that.

MORT: It is another of the more difficult to understand. And the story is pretty much as you said. The owner of the vineyard hired various people in town to work in his field. Some of them worked eight hours, some five, some three and some only one. But at the end of the day they all got paid one dollar, even the ones who'd worked longer than the others.

JANE: That sure doesn't seem fair.

MORT: The workers who'd worked the longest didn't think so, either. But, remember, this is a parable - meant to teach a lesson. What Jesus is really saying is that God is very generous and he will allow into his kingdom both those who had been serving him all their lives as well as those who'd only later in their lives begun to follow him. It is their devotion that matters. And how do you put a price on devotion?

MACK: Do you have a favourite parable, Mort?

MORT: Yes, I like the one where Jesus referred to the apostles as the salt of the earth. I like it for a lot of reasons one of which the clue it gives us about Judas and something he did at the Last Super.

MACK: Tell us about it, Mort.

MORT: During the time Jesus lived, salt was as valuable as gold because, among other things, it preserved food and made it useable. And salt by itself is necessary for life.
If we had no salt, we would die.

JANE: So why were the apostles the salt of the earth?

MORT: Because just as salt purifies and preserves so did the apostles in regard to the rest of humanity. That was their job. To try to purify humanity of its evil.

MACK: And what about Judas?

MORT: Ah, yes. Well in the times of Jesus there was a common expression ***to betray the salt*** which meant to betray one's master. At the Last Supper one of the clues that Judas was the betrayer of Jesus was that he spilled the salt at the table.

JANE: Phew, Mort! This Christianity is hard stuff to practice.

MORT: Tell that to Jesus. Look what he went through.

DIRK: And you guys really think that this Jesus was real?

JACK: Can you prove he wasn't?

DIRK: A guy who was crucified and buried and arose from the dead! Sure I can prove he wasn't real. No one can rise from the dead. You guys as vultures should know that better than anybody.

JANE: But there were witnesses. People saw Jesus after he arose from the dead.

DIRK: I didn't. Anyway, what makes more sense - that a person rises from the dead or that his followers run off with his body and hide it?

MORT: The tomb was under twenty-four hour guard.

DIRK: Guards can be bought off. Witnesses, too, for that matter.

JANE: I don't think we're getting anywhere with Dirk.

MORT: Let me ask you something, Dirk. What if all of the things about Jesus were predicted to happen thousands of years before they did happen? What would you say to that?

DIRK: Coincidence.

MORT: When do too many coincidences add up to conscious planning?

DIRK: When I say so!

With that an angry and frustrated Dirk took a running start and leapt skyward, leaving the argument he couldn't win behind him.

MACK: A typical atheist. Not enough faith to keep up the battle.

MORT: Well said, Mack.

And the three vultures broke from their lesson again and finished the carrion around them like vultures do by nature.

A SHORT BREAK

It is time for a break of our own, but we won't forget Jesus. In fact, we are going to hunt for Jesus. Not with a handgun, of course, but with a camera.

Visions of Jesus pop up all over the world. We're going to show a collection of pictures taken of such sightings purely for entertainment.

Are they really the Lord? I don't think it's likely that he would appear in most of the places he's been seen; he's got more class than that. But it is fun to look at the likenesses of Jesus that have appeared in strange places.

Why do they appear? How do they appear? Often it's just a trick of the light and overactive imagination. But maybe...just maybe someday when we least expect it...

JESUS IN ODD PLACES

Is Jesus in the middle of this mailbox?

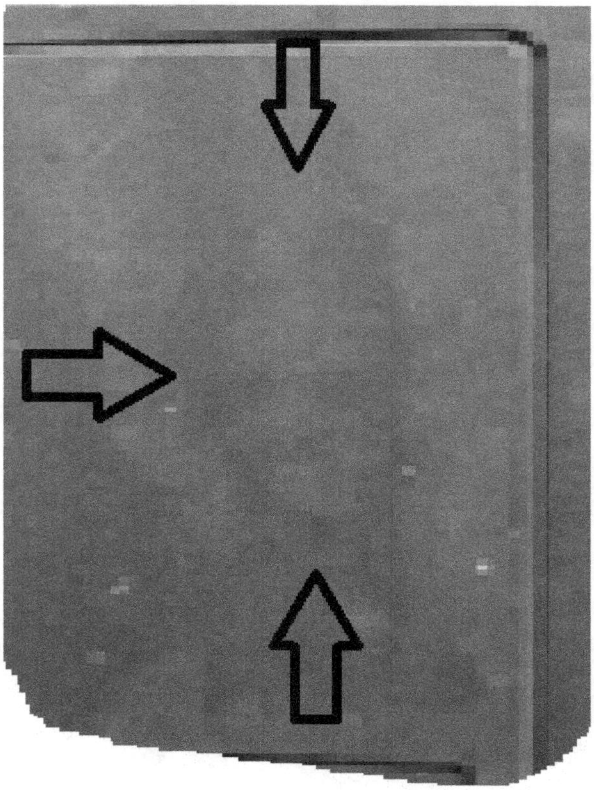

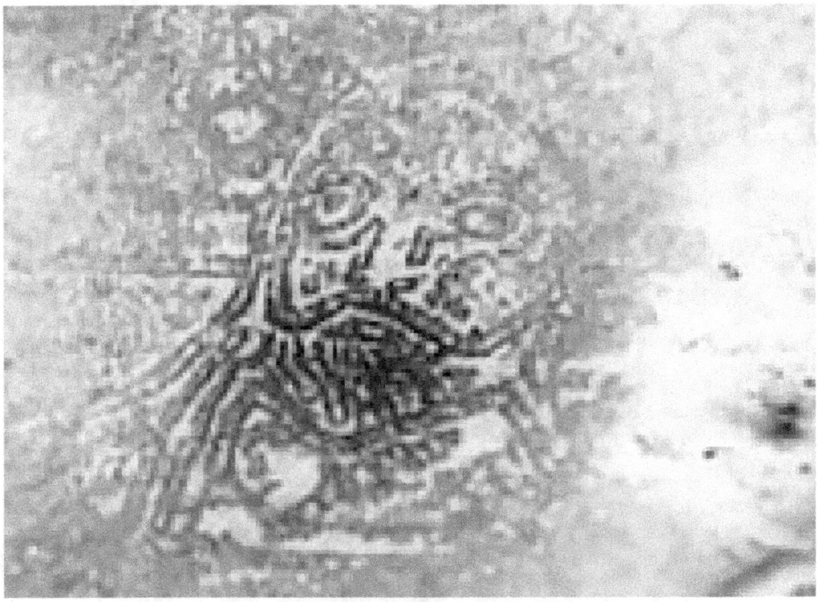

WAIT! JESUS ON A PANCAKE?

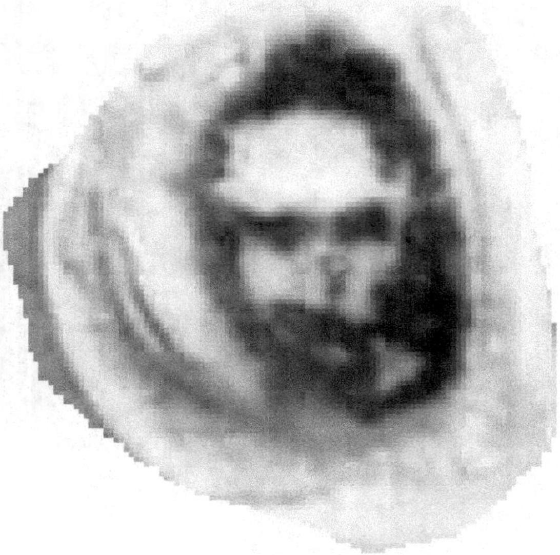

ON A PIROGE?

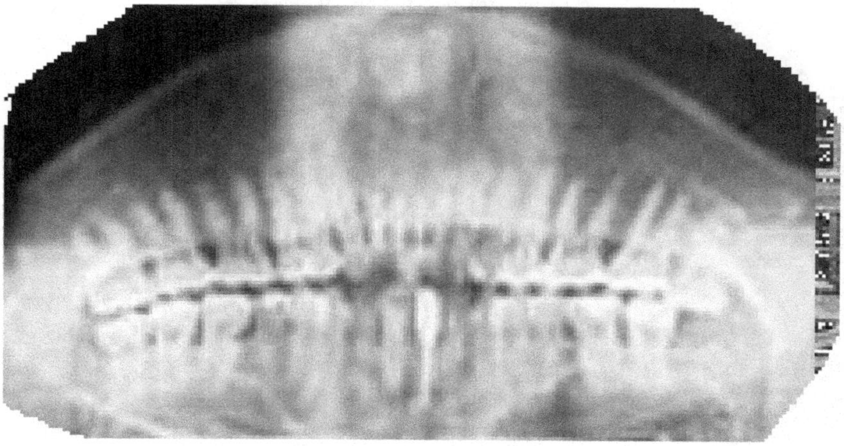

XRAYS REVEAL JESUS IN THE TEETH

JESUS AS A STAIN ON A WALL?

JESUS AS AN ALLUVIAL SAND DEPOSIT

JESUS IN A CLAM SHELL?

ON TOAST?

Just recently - too recent for pictures yet - someone put three pieces of Canadian bacon in their frying pan and when they turned the pieces over the word G O D was burnt into them a letter at a time. Like this:

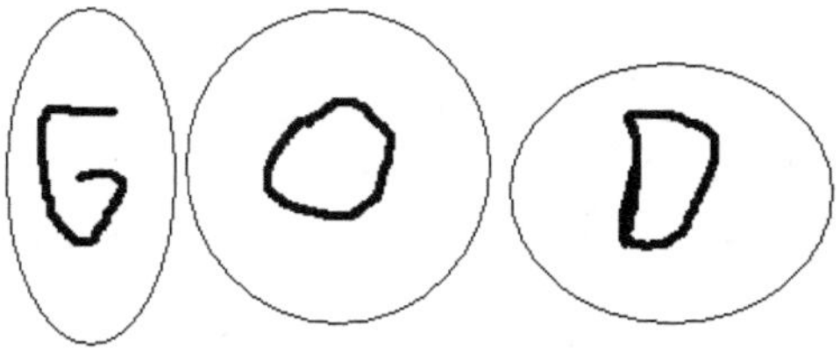

Does anyone really think that God would try to contact them by burning his initials into pieces of ham? Or that Jesus would appear as a stain on a wall?

But at least people are looking for him! And that really is the point of this book - finding Jesus.

HOW TO IMPRESS JESUS

WHAT IF JESUS APPEARED IN YOUR CHURCH ONE DAY?

This isn't a trick question. What if Jesus did show up in your church during services? What would happen?

Just such a thing is said to have happened in a church in Oakland, California. The following stories are taken from a book called "Curses and Ghosts in the Bible."

A former pastor of the Pentecostal Holiness Church in Oakland, California claimed a close encounter with Jesus in April of 1954. During a late Sunday night service while the pastor preached to a congregation of about fifty people an eerie, shadowy form appeared on the glass door which led into the church from outside.

The door opened and a tall, bearded man who fit the description of Jesus Christ entered. He strolled down the central aisle, smiling and blessing the people he passed, and then joined the minister on the speaker's platform. The Jesus look-alike placed a hand on the pastor's shoulder, apparently causing the preacher to faint. The figure knelt beside him, spoke to him in a foreign language which the minister somehow understood, then vanished.

Five years later, a similar event occurred in the same church. On a day in May in 1959 one of the female members of the church took the pulpit to talk about the just described event. She disappeared and was replaced by the form of Jesus. He revealed his palms to the crowd of almost two hundred stunned people, displaying the signs of His crucifixion. Someone in the crowd had a movie camera and caught it all on film. Jesus - or his counterpart - visited for only a short time before disappearing and being replaced by the female speaker who had no recollection of where she had gone.

The film of the event was viewed by many but has mysteriously disappeared.

Do the two preceding occurrences qualify as apparitions of Jesus? They seem very suspicious. Why? They have the appearances of well-planned hoaxes, meaning that the events occurred as if in a staged manner.

In regard to the second event: how did the person who played the part of Jesus vanish? And where did the female church member go when Jesus appeared in her stead? And what about the film?

Magicians have many ways to make a person vanish, as well as replace one object on a stage with another object. Maybe it was all a magician's trick.

Isn't the proof on the film? Not any more - if it ever was. Even the mysterious disappearance of the film is very hoax-like. It's also very reminiscent of all the UFO films and photographs that had suddenly vanished.

But the most difficult aspect to reconcile with true ghostly activity between these two Jesus sightings and the biblical ones is the way that the supposed Jesus acted. Compare how He interacted with the people in the church with the way He interacted with those he encountered shortly after His crucifixion.

The person who entered the church in the guise of Jesus lacked the openness and naturalism of the Jesus who appeared to the disciples. It was as if he were performing on cue and avoiding any attempt at close contact with anyone except those who were part of the script for fear that his true identity would be revealed.

It's highly doubtful that the person who made the two appearances at the Pentecostal Holiness Church was apparitions of the real Jesus.

There is another apparition of Jesus of note which occurred in modern day China. What makes it particularly interesting is that it is an apparent case of time shifting where an event of the past is replayed before a contemporary audience.

It took place before a large, non-Christian group of would-be converts to whom the gospel was being preached. Fortunately, the event was witnessed by an assistant to a U.S. Congressman who was on a fact finding mission to China at the time. Otherwise the occurrence would probably never have been exposed to the world.

While the gospel was being preached, a scene from the past was projected onto the air. The passion of Jesus was displayed before the onlookers as if by miraculous design. This would certainly qualify as a ghostly apparition since in form it was exactly like more common hauntings in which images of the past are depicted on the air.

It seems that Jesus does still make appearances in the world but at only select locations and extremely rarely. Since ascending into heaven, His appearances also are of a different nature, more like images replayed in the ether rather than as an interactive spirit.

There is one thing that we must always remember: JESUS SAID HE WAS COMING BACK. But only the Father knows when.

A DOVE STORY

Mack, Jane and Mort are back.

MORT: I understand that the two of you have a deep interest in the Holy Ghost.

MACK: We sure do, Mort. He is one of the reasons we got so interested in Christianity; because he's a bird like us.

JANE: Or is that just make believe? Do they depict the Holy Ghost as a dove just so people can understand the idea of him easier?

MORT: Actually - no. When the Holy Ghost first appeared to humanity it was in the actual form of a dove.

JANE: That's a relief to hear. But when was it that the Holy Ghost first appeared?

MORT: When John the Baptist baptized Jesus in the Jordan River.

MACK: Isn't that when the voice of God shouted down from the heavens that this was his son in whom he was well pleased?

MORT: Yes, or words to that effect. And as God was making that announcement the Holy Ghost appeared directly above Jesus in the form of a dove.

JANE: Why a dove? Why not a cardinal or a parrot?

MORT: Only God can really answer that. But most theologians think that the dove was used because it's a symbol of peace which harkens back to Noah.

MACK: You mean Noah and the Ark?

MORT: Right. Remember it was a dove that returned after the Flood with an olive branch in its beak to let Noah know that dry land had been located.

JANE: That's right.

MORT: But there's something incredibly amazing about what happened at the baptism of Jesus which most people seem to overlook.

JANE: What, Mort?

MORT: It's one of the extremely rare times when the Holy Trinity is gathered together in one spot at the same time in three different forms.

MACK: I never thought of that.

MORT: Imagine: God the Father is speaking from heaven while his Son is being baptised below with the Holy Ghost hovering just above him.

JANE: Are there other times when the dove made an important appearance?

MORT: Are you kidding! Yes, the Holy Ghost in dove form appeared at some of the most important events in Christianity. One was of particular importance.

JANE: Which one was that?

MORT: He's credited with being the true father of Jesus.

JANE: What!

MORT: That's right. He fathered Jesus.

MACK: And you said that the Holy Ghost did even other things?

MORT: You've heard of Pentecost? That is the day when the Holy Ghost broke in on the apostles shortly after the crucifixion of Jesus. At first, they were terrified. They thought the Romans had come to arrest them.

MACK: Right, they were all hiding.

MORT: This is when the Holy Ghost basically flew into their room as a glowing, radiant white dove. And this is when he gave the apostles the special knowledge that they would need to carry the teachings of Jesus to the world.

JANE: When they learned to speak in tongues.

MACK: Boy, that must've really been scary. Is that why they call him the Holy Ghost, because he scared the apostles like a ghost might?

MORT: No, I don't think so. But...maybe.

JANE: If he is a dove, why is he called a Holy Ghost?

MORT: That is a very difficult question to answer. I have my own personal opinion which may or may not be right.

MACK: Okay, what is it?

MORT: In ancient times an unusual rush of wind was considered the passage of a ghost. I believe that because when the Holy Ghost made his presence known it was often either like or accompanied by a rushing of wind.

JANE: What do you think about calling him the Holy Spirit?

MORT: That's a pet peeve of mine. I don't like it. I think it's just a way to make him sound more acceptable, more glamorous. The Holy Ghost is more descriptive and it's more accurate.

JANE: How do you figure that?

MORT: Well, the idea of a spirit to me is more of a generic, non-personal being. But a ghost is a specific entity. And the Holy Ghost is, I think, like a reflection of God the Father and Jesus but with his own unique personality.

JANE: I like that.

MORT: I like to look at it like this: God sets down the laws, Jesus shows us how to follow them, and the Holy Ghost gives us the inspiration to follow them the right way.

MACK: Wow, Mort! That capuchin taught you well.

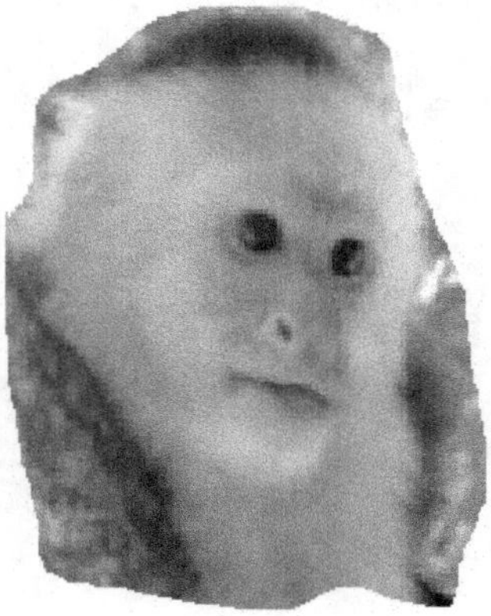

MORT: You two seem to be awfully interested in ghosts. So I think I'll go ahead and tell you a ghost story straight from the Bible.

JANE: Hold on. You mean there are ghost stories in the Bible?

MORT: A lot of them if you know where to look and how to interpret them.

MACK: Can you give us an example?

MORT: Sure. One great example is the Transfiguration of Jesus.

JANE: That's a ghost story?

MORT: Sure. And there's a lot of witnesses to it, too. That's very important.

MACK: I remember something about it. Jesus led Peter, James and John into the mountains and that's when Jesus became all aglow in white.

MORT: Right. And Jesus saw the ghosts - or spirits - of Moses and Elijah. And they had a long conversation.

JANE: So you're saying that Jesus saw two ghosts on this mountain?

MORT: Yes, and so did Peter, James and John. They wanted to build tents for each of them. But then something else happened. God appeared in the holy cloud called the Shekinak and announced again that Jesus was his Son and that he should be listened to.

MACK: So there were a lot of witnesses to what happened.

MORT: Actually, that's a very important part of the Transfiguration. It fulfilled an Old Testament law from the Book of Deuteronomy (19:15) where three witnesses were needed to attest to an event or a fact.

JANE: And the fact was that Jesus was the Son of God and a divine being.

MORT: Right. And also the fact of the Transfiguration itself and the ghostly visions that happened during it.

MACK: Whew! That is pretty spooky.

MORT: So is the time when Saul had the Witch of Endor raise the ghost of Solomon for him.

JANE: Yeah, I heard of that, too.

MORT: If that isn't a sure sign that ghosts are real I don't know what is. It's right there in the Bible.

MACK: But I thought there were rules in the Bible against going to witches and raising the dead.

MORT: There are. But that only confirms the reality of ghosts. If ghosts didn't exist, why would there be a law against raising them?

JANE: Maybe the law was just against TRYING to raise them.

MORT: That may be so. But it is a fact that the Witch of Endor did raise a ghost for Saul. It's documented in the Bible.

JANE: You do have a point there.

MACK: Since we're talking about scary stuff, I'm really confused about something else. After Jesus was crucified, did he descend into Hell?

MORT: That's something that confuses a lot of people and you're going to need a lot more detailed explanation than I can give you.

At this point, Mort suggested that he get them a pamphlet on the topic of Jesus and his descent into Hell. However, we will go into that subject in detail right now.

THE DAY THAT JESUS VISITED HELL

Satan's worst nightmare

This is one of the most misunderstood passages about Jesus and his activities. Look at all the questions it raises:

DOES HELL EXIST?

DID HE REALLY VISIT HELL?

COULD HE VISIT HELL?

WHY WOULD HE VISIT HELL?

WAS SATAN WAITING FOR HIM WITH A PITCHFORK?

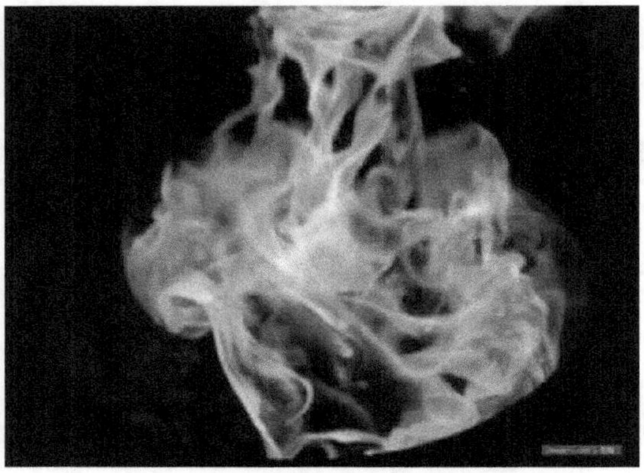

The Apostle's Creed speaks of Our Lord's descent into hell.

First Latin version

Apostle's creed

Credo in Deum Patrem omnipotentem, Creatorem caeli et terrae, et in Iesum Christum, Filium Eius unicum, Dominum nostrum, qui conceptus est de Spiritu Sancto, natus ex Maria Virgine, passus sub Pontio Pilato, crucifixus, mortuus, et sepultus, **descendit ad ínferos**, tertia die resurrexit a mortuis, ascendit ad caelos, sedet ad dexteram Patris omnipotentis, inde venturus est iudicare vivos et mortuos. Credo in Spiritum Sanctum, sanctam Ecclesiam catholicam, sanctorum communionem, remissionem peccatorum, carnis resurrectionem, vitam aeternam. Amen.[9]

Each denomination has its own version of the Apostle's Creed and they are all very similar. A major point where they differ is the part where, in the early Latin version, the creed states that Jesus was "crucified, died, was buried, **descended into Hell**, and on the third day he arose again..."

Later versions changed "descended into Hell" into "descended to the dead" or it was left out completely.

Obviously, descended to the dead isn't nearly the same as descended into Hell. Descended to the dead doesn't really explain anything, does it?

It could just mean Jesus went to a cemetery and checked out the plots.

Descending into Hell is a lot different idea and a lot longer of a trip.

Question: Does Hell exist?

Answer: Yes.

Question: How do you know?

Answer: Because Jesus said so.

A N D

This sign says so.

We know that Hell exists, but where is it? One place we know it **<u>isn't</u>** is in Michigan because it's too cold for Hell in Michigan.

In the 18th century it was commonly believed by many people that Hell was on or in the sun. The problem with that idea is the line in the Apostle's Creed says that Jesus **descended** into Hell. That implies he went downward. I don't think anybody believes that you go down to the sun. Not any more likely than going down to the attic.

Is Hell actually in the bowels of the earth? Science tells us that due to the increasing pressure the farther that one descends the hotter and more intolerable conditions become. Can there really be a physical Hell below? Maybe. No one can really survive a trip that deep into the earth to come back with an answer - assuming Satan would let a person leave.

Wherever Hell really is, Jesus went there. This doesn't make sense to a lot of people. Many believe that by Jesus going to Hell he would give joy to those who were sentenced there to suffer torment.

Actually, just the opposite happened, except for those whose time there was meant to be limited. Among those would be Adam, some of the saints, and those people whose only vice had been Original Sin.

It was exactly because of those people that Jesus visited Hell. These were the people who had not been pure enough to be allowed into heaven, but who - now that Jesus had defied death - could be released from temporary punishment.

Satan knew that Jesus was coming. Prior to Our Lord's arrival the Master of Lies marched about his domain fuming about all of the times that Jesus had overcome him on earth. Satan recalled all the demons Jesus had chased out of the souls of the innocent they had possessed. About all of the people he'd caused to suffer from so many diseases that Jesus cured. How Jesus had raised Lazarus from the dead. How Jesus had stood strong against all of Satan's temptations during his time in the desert.

Now Jesus was dead like any other human. And Satan thought that he would be able to torment Jesus once he arrived in Hell.

But that wasn't to be the case. When Jesus appeared he was ablaze in the light of purity. The power of the brightness was so intense that it was torment to Satan and all of the other demons. In fact, they were terrified by the sight of Jesus.

Jesus descended into Hell to show that he had broken the power of Lucifer. He went to Hell because his human part required that he do so like other humans had had to. He could not claim any special godly privileges. The whole point was that he was a man who had arisen from the dead.

And his other main purpose was to release those souls already mentioned. Now that he had defeated death it no longer could hold prisoner those whose only fault had been Original Sin, that first mistake made by Adam and Eve.

Instead of punishing Jesus, Satan begged him to leave because the power of his righteous light was unbearable.

From where did this idea of Jesus descending into Hell come? Most probably it originated with 1 PETER 3: 18-20 where the partial verse reads "...in which also coming he preached to those spirits that were in prison..." These would be the spirits of the deceased who were confined to Hell specifically until Jesus could come and release them.

But nowhere is it clear where Jesus went after his work in Hell was finished. We know one thing, he sure didn't stay around and talk over old times with Satan.

Where does the detailed information about the time Jesus spent in Hell come from? A little known writing called the Gospel of Nicodemus which was written while experiencing a vision of Jesus.

Another very important piece of information was also provided by this gospel: the identity of the two witnesses in Revelation who will be murdered by the Anti-Christ. According to the gospel, they will be Enoch and Elias (or Elijah).

It will be remembered that these two figures never suffered normal death. Enoch was taken directly into heaven by God and Elijah was taken to heaven on a fiery chariot. But the Anti-Christ will kill them when they return to earth during the Last Days. And, like Jesus, they will be allowed to resurrect to heaven after three days.

Not everyone accepts the validity of the Gospel of Nicodemus, so be aware of that problem. But it does explain a lot of things.

There is something from the Old Testament that should be added here: writings from Hosea. He is one of the Bible's very interesting prophets partly because he seems to be overlooked by many but mainly because his prophetic statements are highly significant and straight to the point.

Hosea 6:2 (NIV) After two days he will revive us; on the third day he will restore us, that we may live in his presence.

He explains the time frame involved which had always bothered many people about Jesus descending into Hell. It had to have been sometime after his burial but somehow before the third day.

Hosea's observation I believe gives much more validity to the idea that Jesus did descend into Hell. And there are other points of prophecy which speak of how Jesus would lead the prisoners out of darkness, which seems like what he did when he descended into Hell. The evidence is mounting in favour of this unusual journey that Jesus took.

Hell, of course, would be filled with some pretty horrifying demons. With this thought in mind, a little break is in order, so at this point we will do some:

SATAN SPOTTING

It's just for fun. Below will be a group of depictions of Satan (?) from various sources. You know what a copycat Satan so some sources are like the ones of Jesus.

A little hard to see. Satan on toast. He was probably burnt up because Jesus was on toast first.

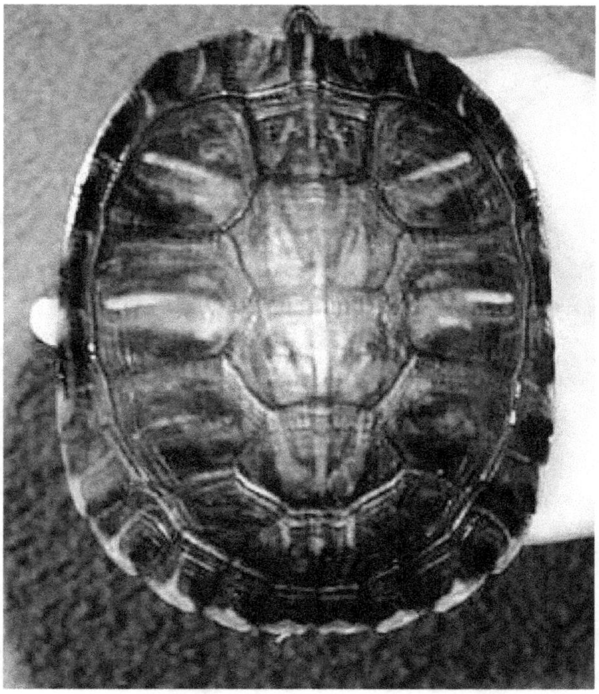

We saw Jesus on a clam. This is Satan on a turtle's back (freeloader).

In a more serious vein. The face a Satan can be seen by some people in these plumes of smoke.

That's a good old-time devil!

Well? Back to Marty Feldman?

VULTURES DEBATE MESSIANIC PROPHECY

JANE: We've always heard that the coming of Jesus was foretold in the Old Testament.

MORT: That's right. There are many prophecies that were filled by Jesus.

DIRK: You guys really believe that? I'll bet anybody can randomly fill most of the prophecies, even me.

MORT: I know one right off that you couldn't fill.

DIRK: What's that?

MORT: I'll bet you weren't a virgin birth.

DIRK: Bah! There's no real proof that Jesus was, either.

MORT: It was foretold in Scripture.

DIRK: I heard of another person who was also supposed to have been a virgin birth, Apollonius. And his father was supposed to be a god, too, a shape-shifting God named Proteus.

MORT: Yes, I know of him. Where might I find the prophecy of his virgin birth?

DIRK: I don't know of any place. But what about your Jesus?

MORT: There are many places, but look up Isaiah Chapter 7 verse 14.

DIRK: Later.

MORT: And when you do, also take a look at Micah 5:2 because it tells where Jesus would be born.

DIRK: Okay, so that might be one or two, that might have been right. Just coincidence.

MORT: Let's see, right after Jesus was born his parents had to take him to Egypt for a little while but came back home soon. That was predicted to happen.

DIRK: Ah, you're probably making that up.

MORT: Nope. I've got the Scripture right here from Hosea 11:1 "When Israel was a child, I loved him, and out of Egypt I called my son."

DIRK: Come on, those could apply to anybody.

JANE: All of them, Dirk. From what I hear, Jesus fulfilled one after another of the prophecies. That's not coincidence or random.

DIRK: You need to be more specific than that.

MORT: Okay, Dirk, here's specific. It was prophesied that the Messiah would come from the house of David, would be born in Bethlehem, and die by crucifixion. Will you accept that without me having to quote the exact scripture?

DIRK: I'll take your word for it, yes.

MORT: Do you know what the odds are for those three things to have happened by sheer chance?

DIRK: No, do you?

MORT: Yes, a mathematician worked out the formula and the odds would be one in 500 billion.

DIRK: Five hundred billion?

MORT: That's right.

DIRK: Still, it is possible.

JANE: Come on Dirk. Use some common sense.

DIRK: Look what you're asking me to believe is pretty outrageous. You're going to need some overwhelming facts to prove your case.

MORT: All right, I have more. A lot more. It was prophesied that Jesus would speak in parables, from Psalms 78:2 *I will open my mouth in parables, I will utter hidden things, things from of old.* It was prophesied that his close friend, Judas, would betray him in Psalms 41:9 - *Even my close friend, whom I trusted, he who shared my bread, has lifted up his heel against me.* It was prophesied that he would be given

vinegar to drink while on the cross in Psalms 69:21- *They put gall in my food and gave me vinegar for my thirst.* It was prophesied that Jesus would verbally commit his spirit into God's hands in Psalms 31:5- *Into your hands*
I *commit my spirit; redeem me, O Lord, the God of truth.* It was prophesied that not one of his bones would be broken in Psalms 34:20-*he protects all his bones, not one of them will be broken.* It was prophesied in Psalms 22:18 that they would cast lots for his garments - *They divide my garments among them and cast lots for my clothing.*

DIRK: All right already.

MORT: And those prophesies were only from Psalms. There are many many more. But so far in total I have given you more than eight prophecies that were clearly fulfilled by Jesus. Do you agree?

DIRK: Yes.

MORT: Another mathematician - named Peter W. Stoner - has discovered that the odds against one person randomly fulfilling eight prophecies is 10,000 trillion trillion.

DIRK: Okay, you may have a point there. But what if someone who lived after Jesus had changed all of the texts in the Scriptures to make sure that he fulfilled these many prophecies?

MORT: Impossible, Dirk. It is authenticated fact that much of the old Testament was written well before Jesus lived.

DIRK: Okay, so then, Jesus was obviously an expert in Scripture, maybe he just read what some of the prophecies were and knew which ones he had to fulfill.

MORT: He could have done that for a few of them, a very few. How could he have arranged his own virgin birth, arranged for the soldiers to cast lots for his garments, prevented the breaking of any of his bones during his crucifixion or arranged his own crucifixion for that matter?

Dirk became silent. He'd run out of objections and arguments. The truth was what it was.

DIRK: Look, I've got to think about this a little more.

With that, Dirk took a running start and leapt skyward.

MORT: I think he's convinced.

JANE: I know I am.

MORT: Now the Holy Ghost will help Dirk to figure things out.

DID YOU EVER WONDER.....

Shortly after the resurrection of Jesus he appeared to the apostles by the Sea of Galilee. They at first did not recognise him.

They were all feeling pretty miserable and even their fishing had taken a turn for the worse. They pulled in only empty nets this sad morning.

The strange looking Jesus approached them and suggested that they cast their nets over the opposite side of the boat. They did as instructed and made a great haul of fish. In fact, there were so many fish in the net that they could barely pull it in.

So, the risen Jesus joined them by their fire and shared a delicious fish and bread breakfast.

...DID JESUS RETURN JUST FOR THE FISH?

DID JESUS REALLY SAY THAT?

During his teachings, Jesus sometimes said some outrageous things. I have a list of some of them below, and have Jesus attired in more casual attire than usual to help take the apparent sting out of some of his words.

Of course, Jesus never meant anything vicious or spiteful in his words. But it seems that there were times when he had to use rather blunt words to get the attention of the less attentive listeners.

He obviously wanted to avoid one of the problems that Paul once had when he spoke at such length one night that one of his younger listeners fell asleep on the ledge of an upstairs window and plummeted to the ground. The young man actually died, but Paul was able - with the grace of God - to revive him.

Matt. 10:34 "Do not suppose that I have come to bring peace to the earth. I did not come to bring peace, but a sword.

Luke 22:36 He said to them, "But now if you have a purse, take it, and also a bag; and if you don't have a sword, sell your cloak and buy one."

A different version: "You must not think that I have come to bring peace to the earth: I have not come to bring peace, but a sword. I have come to set a man against his father, a daughter against her mother, a son's wife against her mother-in-law; and a man will find his enemies under his own roof."

JESUS: PRO-FLOGGING?

In Luke 12:47-48, it states that Jesus says, "The servant who knew his master's wishes, yet made no attempt to carry them out, will be flogged severely. But one who did not know them and earned a beating will be flogged less severely."

JESUS - ANTI-FAMILY MAN

Matthew 12:46-50. "He was still speaking to the crowd when his mother and brothers appeared: they stood outside, wanting to speak to him. Someone said, 'Your mother and your brothers are here outside; they want to speak to you.' Jesus turned to the man who brought the message, and said, 'Who is my mother? Who are my brothers?' and pointing to the disciples, he said, 'Here are my mother and my brothers. Whoever does the will of my heavenly Father is my brother, my sister, my mother.' " Obviously, he didn't speak to them or acknowledge them as his family.

AGAINST GRAVE DIGGERS

Matthew 8:22, It is reported that Jesus says, "Another man, one of his disciples, said to him, 'Lord, let me go and bury my father first.' Jesus replied, 'Follow me and leave the dead to bury their dead.' "

SPREADER OF HATE

Luke 14:26, Jesus states, "If any man come to me, and hate not his father, and mother, and wife, and children, and brethren, and sisters, yea, and his own life also, he cannot be my disciple (a Christian)."

ANIMAL HATER

Matthew 8:28-32, Jesus transferred demons from two men to a herd of innocent pigs, which then jumped over a cliff. Jesus did not even warn the owner of the pigs, or care how it would cost the owner income, or even try to pay the owner for his loss.

I left in some of the negative commentary that was added by non-believers to demonstrate how little they understood Jesus. What the Lord is talking about is how belief in him as the messiah is bound to cause friction in even the most tight knit of families.

Yes, Jesus came with a sword. The sword is used to cut away the powers of Satan not institute a bloodbath on Earth.

The flogging comments are very similar to other parables where he is teaching a lesson.

The pigs became infested with demons and it was the demons who killed the poor animal by diving to their deaths. They could have just as well left the pigs alone just as they can LEAVE US ALONE!

A FINAL LESSON FOR THE VULTURES

Mack, Jane and Mort return and discuss the point of it all.

MACK: Any word on Dirk?

MORT: He's still thinking it over.

JANE: So are we Mort. And the one thing that still bothers me is: what's the purpose of it all? Why did Jesus have to come and die? Who made that rule?

MORT: Great question. It's the one that all Christians have to answer if they are to believe.

MACK: So why did he have to die?

MORT: It starts with Adam and Eve while they were in the garden of Eden.

JANE: Where they committed the first sin by disobeying God.

MORT: Right. And this became the Original sin that all people who came after Adam and Eve also bore.

JANE: But how are we responsible for something Adam and Eve did?

MORT: It's not so much what they did but it's their nature that we share - their tendency toward sin. That is what we inherited simply by being born.

MACK: I see. If you put it that way it makes sense.

JANE: Did God have to punish Adam and Eve? Couldn't he just give them a warning?

MORT: He already warned them. They broke his command not to take the forbidden fruit.

MACK: Still, couldn't he have been lenient. Let it go this first time.

MORT: No, not if he was a just God.

MACK: What?

MORT: It is right that God should punish those that break his rules. If sometimes he does and sometimes he doesn't where does that leave justice?

JANE: So God sent Jesus to be the sacrifice that atoned for the sins of all of us?

MORT: Right.

JANE: Why? Couldn't there have been another solution?

MORT: If there had been, God would have chosen it. The point here is that God has a plan. It is his plan and we can't possibly understand it.

JANE: Sorry if I say so, Mort, but that seems to be an easy answer to a lot of things.

MORT: Maybe so - but it doesn't change the truth. Just like justice, truth doesn't change from day to day.

MACK: One thing we learned we sure can't argue: the whole story of the life of Jesus was prophesied step by step in the Old Testament.

JANE: Yeah, but now we have to wait for him to come again. And we have no idea when that will be.

MORT: Even Jesus can't say when that will be, only the Father.

MACK: If that's true, why do so many people claim to be able to predict his second coming?

MORT: Good question. I can't imagine what these people are thinking. If God the Father did not even tell God the Son when he was being sent back to earth why would any human being think that this information was given to him?

JANE: That is kind of funny, thinking that God won't tell Jesus but he'll tell an average person.

MORT: Anyway, Jesus described what to expect before he comes, the signs to look for. Some of them are pretty scary.

MACK: Like what?

MORT: Jesus said: Nation shall rise against nation and kingdom against kingdom; and great earthquakes shall be in diverse places, and famines and pestilences; and fearful sights and great signs shall there be from heaven.

JANE: Whew!

MORT: For these be the days of vengeance, that all things which are written may be fulfilled. But woe unto them that are with child, and to them that give suck in those days! There shall be great distress in the land, and wrath upon this people.

MACK: You're right, Mort, this is pretty scary.

MORT: Immediately after the tribulation of those days shall the sun be darkened and the moon shall not give her light, and the stars shall fall from heaven and the powers of the heavens shall be shaken. And except that those days be shortened there should no flesh be saved but for the elect's sake those days shall be shortened.

MACK: And then Jesus comes?

MORT: Well, there are a couple of more things you should know about. One of them is the three days of darkness.

JANE: What's that about?

MORT: It's a vision that many respected Christian divines have independently had which tell how during these last days a supernatural darkness will engulf the earth.

JANE: What do you mean by supernatural?

MORT: Not a normal type of darkness. It will be absolute. And the only light will come from blessed candles. Nothing else on earth will give off light. And in the darkness demons and satanic monsters will be roaming and viciously murdering anything they come upon.

JANE: I didn't know it would get this scary.

MORT: But there's good news.

MACK: You mean even during these bad times?

MORT: Yes, it's called the rapture. That's when the faithful followers of Jesus will be transported from the earth to safety so they will not have to suffer through these horrific times.

MACK: I don't quite understand that.

MORT: You have friends who ware ducks, don't you?

MACK: Uh, yeah, a couple of Wood ducks.

MORT: Do they ever know when duck hunting season will start?

MACK: No, they're ducks. They only know hunting season has started by the gunshots directed at them.

MORT: Right. Now what if someone came along and warned these ducks that hunting season was about to start and showed them a place where they could safely wait it out?

MACK: I see. That's kind of what the rapture is like.

JANE: But will it work for us?

MORT: It will work for any faithful Christian.

JANE: Whew! That is good news.

MACK: And good reason to be a faithful follower of Jesus.

MORT: Fear of punishment is not necessarily a bad thing if it brings positive results.

Suddenly, Mort, Jane and Mack look skyward to see the return of an old friend.

MACK: Hey, it's Dirk!

MORT: Maybe he's got a message for us.

Dirk lands and joins the other three vultures.

JANE: Hey, Dirk, you're back! Good to see you again.

DIRK: I was just wondering if you could tell me some more about Jesus. He's a pretty interesting fellow.

MORT: Be glad to, dirk. Glad to.

It looks like Dirk is well on the way to accepting Jesus into his life. Sometimes it takes years for this to happen, sometimes almost over night. But it's like in the parable about the workers in the vineyard, it isn't the length of time one serves him that Jesus is interested in, it's the depth of devotion.

There is one final task to perform. It involves the timelessness of Christianity and the many facets of its reality. This is going to be demonstrated in a short story which in its way will span the millennia and strike into the future.

At the centre of the story is the Holy Ghost who is having a discussion with a top emissary of Satan's about a most extraordinary problem.

TALE OF THE HOLY GHOST

A STATUS REPORT ON GOD'S PLAN

AN IRISH PUB IN A TIMELESS ZONE

BARKEEP

Hey, O'shea, change the station on the telly! Hurry! The Big Ghost is coming from the church across the street.

O'SHEA

Right away, Mr. O'Ryan.

BARKEEP

You know how he feels about modern t.v. and all that violence and sex.

O'SHEA

I'll see if I can get the cricket channel. Nothing more peaceful than a cricket match.

The Holy Ghost enters through the front door and takes a seat at the bar. He is of indefinite form.

BARKEEP

Top of the day to you, Mr. Ghost.

GHOST

Ah, delightful, a cricket match.
Nothing more relaxing than cricket.
A sport made in heaven. And I should know.

BARKEEP

The usual for you today?

GHOST

Yes, please. What's more heavenly than wine from Dad's vineyards?

BARKEEP

And how are you today?

GHOST

Oh, about the same as everyday.

BARKEEP

Things do change, though, don't

they?

GHOST

Attitudes and perceptions change
but not things like truth and
honour and love.

BARKEEP

What about the way that everybody keeps
fooling around with your name. All
of a sudden you're the Holy Spirit
instead of the Holy Ghost.

GHOST

I guess they thought that it would
sound more respectable.

He points toward the liquor bottles on the shelf.

GHOST

What's so respectable about being
called after one of their names?

BARKEEP

Uh, I'm not sure I follow your meaning. Somebody wanted to call you OLD TURKEY, after that brand?

GHOST

No! Spirit. Those types of drinks are also known as spirits. Being called the Holy Ghost is just fine with me.

BARKEEP

There was a time when you almost didn't even have a name, remember?

GHOST

Remember! Hey, I remember things that never even happened.

BARKEEP

But some people didn't even think you were part of the Trinity, or that there even was a Trinity.

GHOST

I had to...enlighten them. But I've been around since the beginning, way before the Christian era. How about Moses and that Burning Bush?

BARKEEP

That was an absolutely fantastic idea!

GHOST

Dad sure liked it. He does like to pull pranks now and then - what better than to turn himself into a talking bush - a burning one yet.

BARKEEP

You seemed to like doing this type of thing to Moses.

GHOST

You mean like the pillar of fire I whipped up to lead him through the desert?

BARKEEP

Yes, that. You know, you seem to have a fascination with fire.

GHOST

My other 2/3rds noticed that, too, because fire is more in the area of another entity who shall remain nameless. But I reminded the other 2/3rds that we created fire after all and we can do what we like with it.

BARKEEP

You sure were busy back in the day. But it seems like you're not doing so much any more.

GHOST

Are you kidding! Do you know how many confirmations I'm at right now?

BARKEEP

No.

GHOST

Plenty. And do you know how many people I'm causing to talk in tongues right now? Quite a few. And I get thirsty, I tell you, even when I'm talking through someone else.

He finished his drink and holds his glass out for a refill.

GHOST

Can't fly on one wing, you know. Good thing I can burn off that alcohol psychically.

BARKEEP

About flying on one wing. Doesn't it ever bother you that you're depicted as a bird by the Christians?

GHOST

Dove! Not any old bird, a dove!

BARKEEP

I reckon it does bother you.

GHOST

Not really, better a dove than a pelican or a turkey.

BARKEEP

What if they'd seen you as a woman?

GHOST

Since I am a spirit, nobody has really tried to pin any kind of gender on me - really. One thing does make me wonder what our top third was thinking.

BARKEEP

You mean, God?

GHOST

Yes, Him. I mean - you have God the Father, God the Son, and the Holy Ghost as a dove. I guess I'm their pet.

BARKEEP

Ha, you are bothered about being described as a dove.

O'Shea

You better change the subject.

BARKEEP

Tell me, what are your other 2/3rds doing these days now that Christianity has pretty well rooted?

GHOST

Well, the first third of us is watching over the universe, making sure everything is working the way he wants it. And my other third: he's on another planet, getting Christianity started there. I'll have to be going there to help him out pretty soon.

BARKEEP

When's he going to be coming back here again?

GHOST

Trade secret. I can't tell you that.

BARKEEP

He IS coming back, isn't he?

GHOST

He said he was. I've never known him to lie.

Their talk is interrupted as O'Shea notices another special patron approaching the pub.

O'SHEA

We better get ready. Here comes Archduke Azmodeus, one of Satan's top men.

BARKEEP

Big Ghost, you don't mind if I turn off the telly, do you? Azmodeus will want to watch the latest disasters on the news and that always causes a row.

GHOST

Sure, turn it off in the name of peace.

BARKEEP

Thanks for understanding.

GHOST

Ha, I can keep watching cricket in my head as long as I want to.

A shadowy figure enters and takes a seat next to the Holy Ghost.

BARKEEP

What will it be for you today, Azzy?

ASMODEUS

Same as usual, stout beer

BARKEEP

Aye, sir, coming right up.

AZMODEUS

Nothing on the telly?

BARKEEP

Tis broken.

AZMODEUS

Ha! I like it when you lie to me.

You're really afraid that I'll watch the news and get all rowdy because things are going so well for my side. All types of murders and killings and blood spilling.

GHOST

Only for now.

AZMODEUS

Why, if it isn't the Holy Ghost! I haven't seen you since I don't know when.

GHOST

Of Course not, I never let you. But I come in here about everyday.

AZMODEUS

Looks like your side isn't doing so well these days. Satan's got the upper hand now. He's been pretty happy these days.

GHOST

Not like the Middle Ages, huh?

AZMODEUS

He was a terror to live with then. His only consolation was the plague and all of those popes who came over to our side.

GHOST

What kind of people are you getting these days down there?

AZMODEUS

Mostly your common killers and that sort, nobody remarkable.

GHOST

Not a lot of Hitlers lately.

AZMODEUS

No, but ones like him only come along once in an age. But, you know, one of our newcomers has presented the Master quite a problem. It must've been providence that brought us together today.

GHOST

Providence? Do you think Our Father had something to do with it?

AZMODEUS

Well, you always are telling people how He works in mysterious ways.

GHOST

We didn't suspect that you'd be listening.

AZMODEUS

We've recently had some difficulty with a new arrival.

GHOST

Why tell me?

AZMODEUS

I thought you might find it an interesting problem.

GHOST

Are you trying to tempt me?

AZMODEUS

Tempt you? Heaven forbid!

GHOST

Well put.

AZMODEUS

Come on, you know that temptations aren't my department. That's sales. I'm on the Board of Directors.

GHOST

All right, so what's your problem?

AZMODEUS

This new arrival...we've never had anything like it.

GHOST

Hold on a minute. I just saw an old friend of ours come in.

A woman appearing to be in her mid thirties with waist-length black hair and attired in a floor-length violet sun dress enters the pub and storms up to the bar. She takes a seat between Azmodeus and the Holy Ghost. Her name is Veronica.

VERONICA

Ha! At last I found the two of you together! I've got a few things to say to both of you.

BARKEEP

Can I get you something?

VERNONICA

A tall glass of orange juice.

BARKEEP

With or without pith?

VERONICA

No pits, please.

BARKEEP

No pits either.

VERONICA

Listen you two, there are a lot of souls out there who need you two to clear some things up pretty quickly.

GHOST

And good day to you Veronica.

AZMODEUS

We went through this Epochs ago, Veronica. Do we have to go through it all again?

VERONICA

Yes. Someone has to help those who have been kept out of heaven, or even the other realm, through no fault of their own.

GHOST

Be careful what you ask for. Some of your clients might just rather stay in LIMBO than be sent to damnation.

VERONICA

That's a tired old argument. You know as well as I that none of my clients are damned, otherwise they would already have been sentenced.

GHOST

Look, the way to get to Heaven has

already been laid out. Those who haven't yet qualified will just have to wait a little longer, that's all.

VERONICA

That's all! That's all! Just until the end of time. And when will that be?

AZMODEUS

When time ends, I assume.

There is a sudden flash and two early hominids who looked more like apes than humans appeared near the pool table. They immediately began racking up the balls.

VERONICA

Do you know how long they've been waiting already? About seven million years. And there aren't enough pool tables in LIMBO to go around.

AZMODEUS

Too bad the humans degenerated after Adam and Eve.

VERONICA

Don't confuse things. I need an answer to take back to the souls I'm representing.

GHOST

You claim to talk about justice. Is it just that the souls who have not endured the misery of Earth - like many of those in LIMBO - should be allowed directly into Paradise along with those who had suffered greatly?

AZMODEUS

That's telling her.

VERONICA

Huh, is it just that these innocent souls be made to linger in semi-nothingness due to nothing they did? Some of them didn't even have the chance to be born!!!

GHOST

The unborn will be taken good care of in all good time, along with the others.

And some of them may yet end up
in Satan's realm.

AZMODEUS

Oh, no! We don't need any zombies. We want healthy, vicious souls for our final war.

GHOST

Come on, Azzy, who are you trying to kid? Are you getting that propaganda directly from that Nazi Goebbels?

VERONICA

Speaking of propaganda: why don't you two be realistic and give up the ghost?

GHOST

I beg your pardon?

VERONICA

Quit all these recruiting tactics and let souls lead their own lives. Give them real freedom of choice.

AZMODEUS

Nonsense. We have to recruit to raise our army for the final battle.

GHOST

There isn't any way you could ever beat us. It's like playing a game where we started with one point more than you and will always have one point more.

VERONICA

I particularly don't like your recruitment methods, Azmodeus. Look at what you do: you tempt people with all kinds of snares that get them sent to your realm and then, once they're there, you punish them for following your instructions. That's pretty lousy.

AZMODEUS

As usual, you've got it all wrong. Our goal is to raise an army to reclaim control of all reality. Yes, we do lie to these people to get them here because we want vicious people, people who feel totally betrayed. We want these souls filled with the same fury as Lucifer so they will fill an invincible army.

GHOST

There he goes with that army again!

AZMODEUS

Our side is already destroying your reality. That's what evil does.

GHOST

You're only fooling yourselves. For any destruction we allow you to cause ten additional things come into being.

AZMODEUS

You allow us to cause! What conceit that is.

GHOST

Hardly conceit, Azzy. Fact. You and your master are living in a delusionary reality we created for you.

VERONICA

Hold On, Big Ghost. I think Azzy has a point here. Allowing souls to suffer at the whim of Satan and his stooges makes you just as guilty.

GHOST

If you mean guilty of allowing thinking creatures to have free will and to be able to make bad choices I guess you're right.

VERONICA

Free will again! Huh! No one really has a choice and you know it.

GHOST

Why not?

VERONICA

Uh...I...?

GHOST

The simple fact is that my Dad has a plan from before the beginning and none of you have the slightest idea what it is. And, by the way, it's working perfectly.

AZMODEUS

I'm so sick of hearing of this plan of yours.

GHOST

Not mine - Dad's

AZMODEUS

Yeah, sure, God - your Daddy.

VERONICA

Prove it, Big Ghost. Prove this all knowing all wonderful plan.

GHOST

The proof is all around you in everything around you.

AZMODEUS

Look, I ain't got time for all of this metaphysical chit chat. I had something specific I wanted to talk to the Big Ghost about.

GHOST

Yes, that would be the new arrival that recently came to your realm.

AZMODEUS

Do you know what this thing is that we got delivered to us?

GHOST

Why, don't you?

AZMODEUS

Of course I do. It's a computer!

VERONICA

A computer!

AZMODEUS

Yes, remember the plague that wiped out 85% of the population of Earth at the end of the 23rd century?

VERONICA

Yes, a lot of the dead were un-baptized children who were sent to LIMBO!

AZMODEUS

That strain of plague was completely designed by the mind of one computer, the ELL6.

VERONICA

So? It's just a machine. What're you doing with it.

AZMODEUS

It has consciousness. It has a personality. It is more than a machine, it is a living being with a soul.

GHOST

Is that right? Sounds like Artificial Intelligence.

AZMODEUS

Don't be cute. You're the one who sent him to us.

GHOST

Me. That's not my job. Maybe Saint Peter can help you.

AZMODEUS

Nope, this has all of the earmarks of a Holy Ghost scheme.

VERONICA

Wait a minute. So what if the thing you got delivered is a computer? So?

AZMODEUS

Our job is to torment souls that come to us. How do we torment a computer?

VERONICA

I'd think that would be simple. Feed it a program that sends it into a literal infinite loop.

AZMODEUS

That was the first thing we thought of. This computer loved it. It thrives on being active, even if computing senseless, infinite data. Its purpose is to be active.

VERONICA

But it's a computer. I think you should get another ruling on its assignment to your realm.

AZMODEUS

We already did that. ELL6 knew what it was doing when it created the plague virus, it has a genuine hatred for humans and wanted to kill as many off as possible, it realised it was an evil thing to do and it has absolutely no remorse. It thinks, it feels and it has a soul.

VERONICA

You said that its purpose is to be active. Shut it down, that's all.

AZMODEUS

How do you shut down a soul? This isn't a machine any longer. Its physicality no longer exists.

VERONICA

Then why can't you torment it like you do all of the other poor souls?

AZMODEUS

Because it does not recognise the sensation of pain of any type - mental or physical.

VERONICA

Then I'm stumped.

AZMODEUS

I knew you would be. But it was the Big Ghost whose advice I wanted to ask.

GHOST

It sounds like you do have a problem.

AZMODEUS

Problem! Problem! Satan is delirious. He can't allow any being in his realm whom he can't punish. That makes this creature almost an...equal of his.

GHOST

Yes, quite a dilemma.

AZMODEUS

Yes we already know that.

The Holy Ghost rises and floats toward the door.

GHOST

You wanted proof that our plan was working?

The Holy Ghost vanishes.

AZMODEUS

What did he mean by that?

VERONICA

It looks like they set up your master with a problem he can never solve even if he works all eternity on it.

Azmodeus begins to literally burn with rage. He eventually bursts into a flaming fireball and explodes into nothingness, leaving a pile of ashes on the floor.

BARKEEP

Hey, O'Shea, get the broom. Azmodeus just blew up.

Veronica then finishes her drink and vanishes much more politely.

O'Shea begins sweeping the ashes.

O'SHEA

Well, I guess we won't see them for another few millennia.

BARKEEP

Yep, and that cricket match we had on the telly earlier will probably still be going.

A LAST REMINDER.

FALSE GODS ARE EVERYWHERE! BY LEARNING TO RECOGNISE THEM, YOU CAN AVOID THEM.

IDENTIFY THE FALSE GODS BEFORE LEAVING

AND

ANY

PERSON WHO RULES YOUR

LIFE

BEYOND YOUR CONTROL

OTHER THAN GOD.

BEWARE THE FALSE GODS AND ALWAYS REMEMBER THE GREATEST OF COMMANDMENTS!

FINALLY,

HOW TO IMPRESS JESUS?

Try to love your enemy. Jesus knows how hard that is.

www.ingramcontent.com/pod-product-compliance
Lightning Source LLC
Chambersburg PA
CBHW060516300426
44112CB00017B/2696
* 9 7 8 0 9 3 0 4 7 2 5 1 1 *